Magic
MUD
AND OTHER GREAT EXPERIMENTS

BY GORDON PENROSE

ILLUSTRATED BY TINA HOLDCROFT

A LITTLE SIMON BOOK PUBLISHED BY SIMON AND SCHUSTER INC. NEW YORK

Manufactured in Hong Kong

10 9 8 7 6 5 4 3 2 1
10 9 8 7 6 5 4 3 2 1 (pbk.)

Library of Congress Cataloging-in-Publication Data. Penrose, Gordon. Magic mud and other great experiments. Includes index. Summary: A collection of science activities demonstrating basic scientific principles. 1. Science—Experiments —Juvenile literature. [1. Science—Experiments. 2. Experiments] I. Holdcroft, Tina, ill. II. Title. Q164.P36 1988 507'.8   87-16962 ISBN 0-671-64969-8 ISBN 0-671-65767-4 (pbk.)

CONTENTS

DR. ZED'S EGG-CITING MAGIC

The Great Egg Challenge #1

How can you tell a raw egg from a hard-boiled egg without cracking the shell?

You can't. It's impossible!

Oh no it's not! It just takes a flick of the wrist.

Huh?

How to Solve the Great Egg Challenge # 1

1. Spin both eggs on a table.

2. Stop them quickly, then immediately let go of them.

3. One of the eggs will start spinning again when you let it go. Which one?

The raw egg keeps spinning because the liquid inside it is still moving.

Things you'll need:
two eggs: one hard-boiled, one raw *(they should both be cold)*; **vinegar; jar**

About these experiments:
Dr. Zed explores inertia as well as the effect of acetic acid on calcium carbonate.

How to Solve the Great Egg Challenge # 2

1. Place the hard-boiled egg in a jar and cover it with vinegar.

2. After two hours it should feel soft and rubbery, but if you leave it overnight the shell will have completely disappeared by morning.

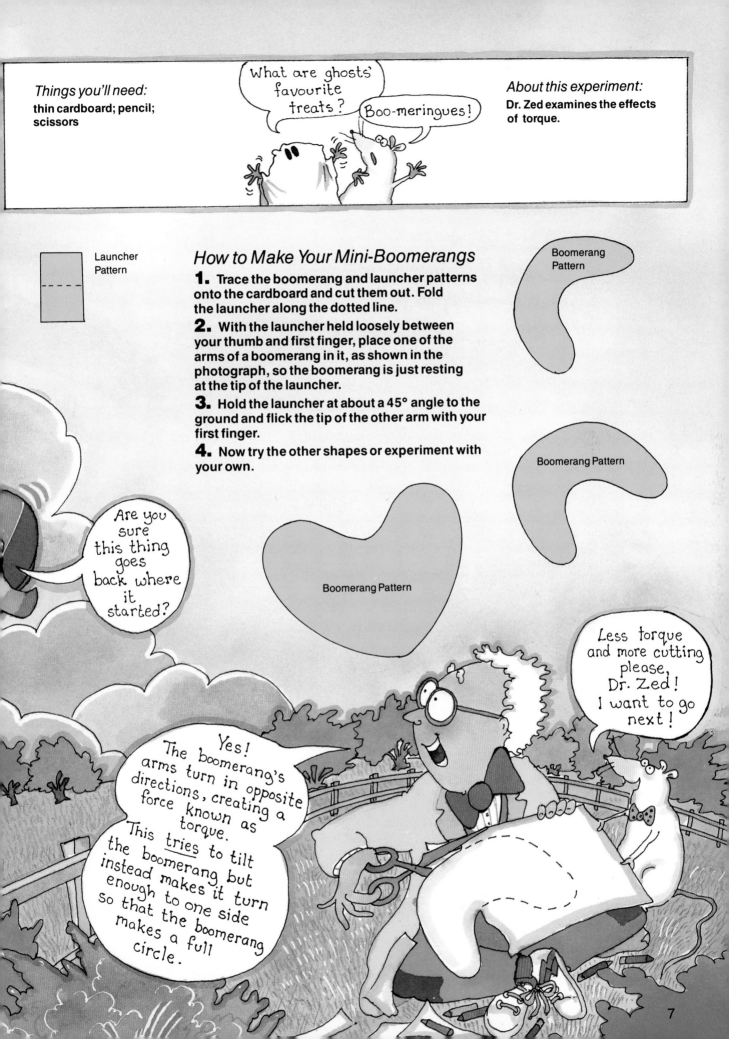

Things you'll need:
thin cardboard; pencil; scissors

What are ghosts' favourite treats?

Boo-meringues!

About this experiment:
Dr. Zed examines the effects of torque.

Launcher Pattern

How to Make Your Mini-Boomerangs

1. Trace the boomerang and launcher patterns onto the cardboard and cut them out. Fold the launcher along the dotted line.

2. With the launcher held loosely between your thumb and first finger, place one of the arms of a boomerang in it, as shown in the photograph, so the boomerang is just resting at the tip of the launcher.

3. Hold the launcher at about a 45° angle to the ground and flick the tip of the other arm with your first finger.

4. Now try the other shapes or experiment with your own.

Boomerang Pattern

Boomerang Pattern

Boomerang Pattern

Are you sure this thing goes back where it started?

Less torque and more cutting please, Dr. Zed! I want to go next!

Yes! The boomerang's arms turn in opposite directions, creating a force known as torque. This _tries_ to tilt the boomerang but instead makes it turn enough to one side so that the boomerang makes a full circle.

7

Things you'll need:
75 mL (5 tablespoons) cornstarch;
45 mL (3 tablespoons) water;
measuring spoon; mug, spoon;
food colouring

About this experiment:
Dr. Zed investigates the properties of a suspension made out of cornstarch.

> Would you care for a glass of colloidal suspension?

> Uh? Looks like milk to me.

> How right you are!

> I love this stuff.

> I can pick up a lump, but then it melts. Why?

> When you press the mud it feels solid because you squeeze out some of the water.
>
> But when you stop squeezing, water flows back again and the mud becomes runny.

How to Make Magic Mud

1. Spoon the cornstarch into the mug.

2. Add the water and stir. It should be difficult to stir, even when the water and cornstarch are fully mixed.

3. Colour your magic mud. N.B. Don't add too much food colouring or your mud will become runny. If this happens, add a little cornstarch until the mud feels like it did in step # 2.

Now Make a Mud Pie

Squeeze a small quantity of magic mud between your fingers and roll it into a ball or sausage. What happens when you stop squeezing the mud?

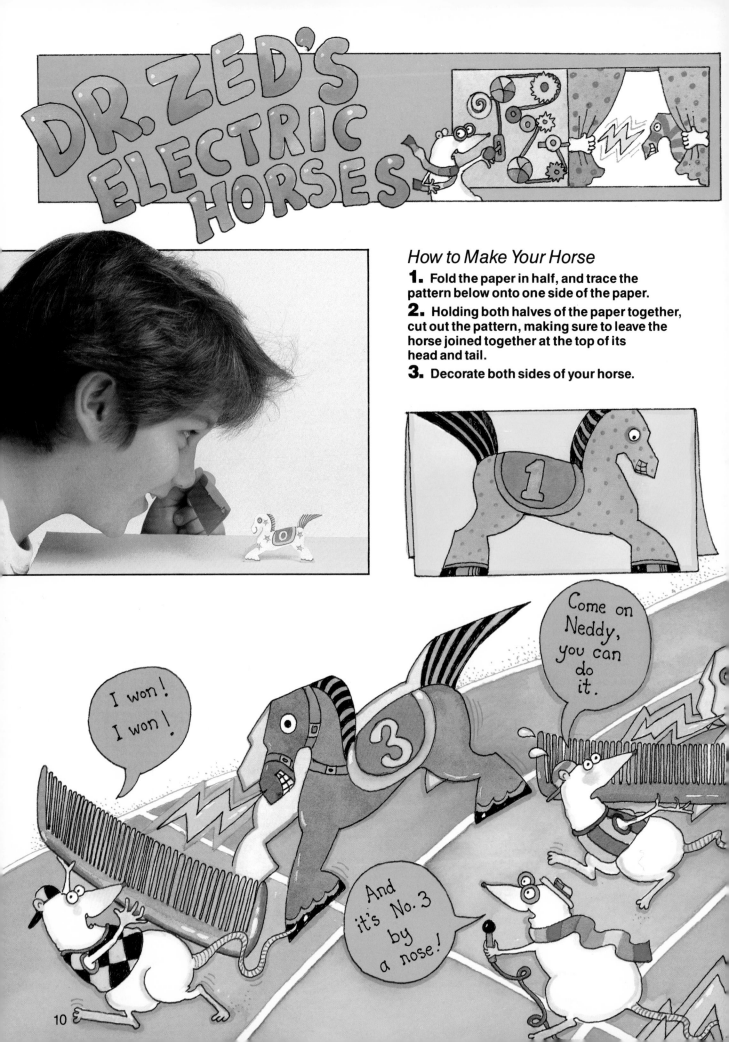

DR. ZED'S ELECTRIC HORSES

How to Make Your Horse

1. Fold the paper in half, and trace the pattern below onto one side of the paper.

2. Holding both halves of the paper together, cut out the pattern, making sure to leave the horse joined together at the top of its head and tail.

3. Decorate both sides of your horse.

How to Electrify Your Horse

Stand your horse on a smooth surface, comb your hair several times and hold the comb in front of the horse's nose — be sure not to touch the comb to the nose. The horse will move towards the comb. Practise until you can pull the horse along without it ever touching the comb.

DR. ZED'S FEATHER FLYER

First Make the Body...

1. Fasten the string to the paper clip.

2. Push the paper clip well into the styrofoam ball.

Then Turn it into a Glider...

1. Stick the feathers into opposite sides of the ball. Adjust them so that they both tilt forwards slightly and curve upwards.

2. Run and pull the glider behind you, and it will glide along at about shoulder height.

3. If your glider won't glide properly, experiment with the tilt of its wings.

Those curved feathers really give the flyer a lift.

Yes, their shape helps the air move fast over their top surface. And, as you know, fast-moving air = lower air pressure = lift.

Oh dear, I knew there was some reason I didn't like heights.

Things you'll need:
two large feathers
(gull feathers work well);
6 cm (2-1/4 inches)
diameter styrofoam ball;
paper clip; string; decorations

Did you know that glider planes use rising, warm air to soar so high?

Big deal! I've been doing that for years.

About this experiment:
Dr. Zed explores Bernoulli's Principle *(as the speed of a liquid or gas increases, the pressure it exerts decreases).*

change the curve of one feather so that it acts as an air brake, and your feather flyer will spin. What would you do to change your flyer into a kite?

Next Turn it into a Propellor
1. Turn one of the wings so that it curves downwards and remove the string.
2. Climb up on a chair or find a stairwell and drop the feather propellor. It will spin to the ground.

About this experiment:

Dr. Zed looks into the reaction of
protein molecules in gelatin to heat
and cold. (It tastes good too.)

How to Make Jelly Pops

1. To make four jelly pops, pour the juice into the pot and sprinkle the gelatin on it. Stir over low heat until the gelatin dissolves (about five minutes).

2. Rinse out the popsicle tray with cold water then fill it with the juice mixture.

3. Cover the tray with aluminum foil and push a stick through it into each mold.

4. Put the jelly pops into the freezer for about two hours. To remove the pops from the tray, dip the tray into hot water and run a knife blade around the mold edges. Enjoy.

DR. ZED'S WATER THREADS

I bet the salt water threads fall because they're heavier than the clear water.

And it says here that a very thin thread of slow-moving water will stick together and not spread out.

DYNAMIC FLUIDS I'VE KNOWN AND LOVED
by Seymour Waters

So why do you get those rings on the

How to Make Water Threads

1. Fill the glass jar with water so that when you fit the container into the neck of the jar, its bottom just sits in the water. Remove the container and let the water in the jar sit for 15 minutes until it is completely still.

2. Use the pin to poke three evenly-spaced holes across the bottom of the container.

3. Pour a 1 cm (1/2 inch) layer of salt into the container, add food colouring to it and stir until the salt is evenly coloured.

4. Replace the container in the neck of the jar. In a short while, thin threads of coloured water should start to stream from the holes in the bottom of the cup. If they don't, check to see if there's an air bubble trapped beneath the container. You can remove this by lifting the container and tilting the jar slightly.

DR. ZED'S GREEN SHEEP

How to Make Your Green Sheep

1. Next time someone in your family is cooking with an egg, ask him or her not to crack it but to empty it by making a hole at its middle.

2. Rinse out the egg shell, dry it and wrap a piece of tape lengthwise around it. Cut the eggshell through the tape as shown.

3. Make sheep legs out of pieces of cotton swabs. Tape the legs and a paper head and tail to the shell.

4. Pack the shell full of absorbent cotton or paper towel. Add water so the cotton or towel is moist but not soaking wet. Sprinkle half a teaspoonful of alfalfa seeds on top and place your sheep in a warm place.

5. Check your sheep twice a day to make sure the cotton or towel is moist. Your sprouts will be ready to snip and eat in five to seven days.

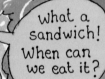

Things you'll need:

stiff cardboard; pencil; ruler;
two pocket mirrors loosely taped
together on their dull sides; straight
pins; disc made out of thin cardboard;
felt-tip pens

Did you know the Kaleidoscope was invented in 1816 by Sir David Brewster?

About this experiment:

Dr. Zed explores the symmetrical arrangement of images in two mirrors in a see-how-it-works kaleidoscope.

1

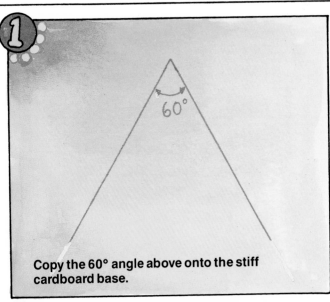

60°

Copy the 60° angle above onto the stiff cardboard base.

2

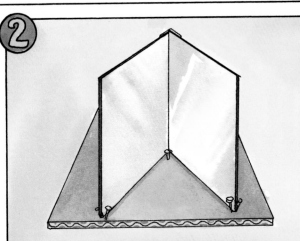

Stand the mirrors on the 60° angle lines and stick the pins in place as shown. Lift the mirrors and the centre pin off the base.

3

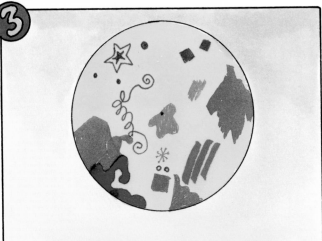

Decorate the disc with coloured shapes and patterns.

4

Assemble the kaleidoscope like this:

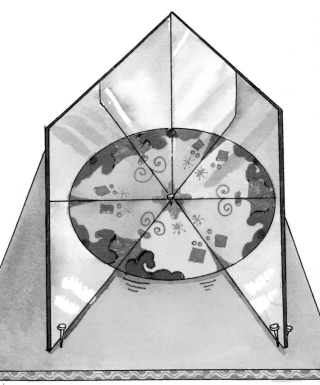

To make it work, twirl the disc with one hand while holding the base with the other.

Wow! With a 60° angle you get six reflections!

Tina Holdcroft

How to Make Your Wind Wheel

1. Glue the two paper plates back to back. Let the glue dry.

2. Use a pencil and ruler to divide one of the plates into eight equal segments as shown.

3. Start at the middle and cut through both plates along each line. *(If you're allowed to use one, a sharp knife or blade works well.)*

4. Fold each point as shown – one towards you, the next away from you and so on.

How to Use Your Wind Wheel

On a windy day, roll your wheel along a smooth sidewalk and watch the wind zoom it away.

Things you'll need:

30 cm x 30 cm (12 inches x 12 inches) square corrugated cardboard; sharp knife; 36 cm x 36 cm x 51 cm (14 inches x 14 inches x 20 inches) triangle brown paper; ruler; decorations

About this experiment:
Dr. Zed examines sound — what it is and how you hear it.

How to Make Your Air Banger

1. Score the front of the cardboard between points A and D, being careful not to cut all the way through. Turn the square over.

2. Place the long side of the paper triangle on the back of the cardboard square between points B and C. Holding the paper in place, flip the square back over *(see diagram)*. **Fold the short sides of the paper triangle over the edge of the cardboard and tape them down securely.**

3. Fold the cardboard in half along the score line so that the paper folds in half inside it.

4. Decorate your air banger.

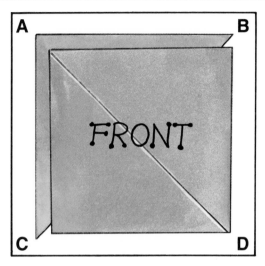

How to Use Your Air Banger

Hold the banger above your head and fling your arm down as hard as you can.

Those shock waves just reached my ears as a loud bang!

When you snap the banger down it forces the air out so fast that the shock waves make the air vibrate.

Tina Holdcroft

Things you'll need:
plasticine; cardboard wrapping paper roll; decorations

About this experiment:
Dr. Zed moves a lever's fulcrum point to create an illusion.

How to Make Your Magic Balancing Wand

1. Divide your plasticine into two chunks, one three times bigger than the other.

2. Plug one end of the roll with the small piece of plasticine; plug the other with the large piece.

3. Add a star, if you wish, to the light end of the wand, then find and mark the wand's balance point. Hint: it's closer to the heavy end of the wand than the other.

4. Decorate your wand, making sure that you still know where the balance point is.

How to Do the Trick

1. If you're right-handed, the heavy end of the wand should be on your right side; opposite for left-handers.

2. Balance the wand on your index finger then slowly and gently roll your finger to one side so that the light end of the wand rises.

3. As you wave your free hand over the light end of the wand, give the command, "Rise Up, O Wand of Zed!" and roll your finger so the light end rises. P.S. Practise first!

How to Make Your Valentine

1. Trace the outline of the two dotted squares and their contents onto the paper.

2. Cut out the two paper squares.

3. Tape one nickel to the top of one side of the cardboard and the other to the bottom of the other side.

4. Tape one paper square to one side of the cardboard. Tape the other one *upside down* on the back of the cardboard.

5. Poke the sharp point of the scissors through the four circles you traced on the paper squares.

6. Cut the string in half. Loop one half through one pair of holes and knot the loose ends together. Do the same with the other half.

Now Put Some Love in Your Heart

1. Hold one loop of string in each hand.

2. Wind up the string by revolving the cardboard.

3. Pull gently on the wound-up string and the cardboard will spin. The word "LOVE" will magically appear between "I" and "YOU" inside the heart.

Aw shucks. How soppy can you get?

DR. ZED'S ANTI-GRAVITY TRICK

Why does the water follow the string, Dr. Zed?

It's the water's surface tension that holds it to the string.

This same force holds water coming out of a tap in a pipe-like shape.

Don't let the string sag or I'll get wet.

Things you'll need:

plastic measuring jug or pitcher with a handle; plastic cup; piece of string as long as your outstretched arms; water

About this experiment:

Dr. Zed explores surface tension in water.

If you put a blue hat into green water what would it be?

Er, um... turquoise?

Try wet!

How to Set Up the Trick

N.B. Perform this trick where it won't matter if you spill a little water.

1. Wet the string and tie one end of it to the handle of the pitcher.

2. Stretch the string over the spout of the pitcher and let the loose end drop into the cup, which you are holding directly below.

3. Hold the loose end of the string against the inside of the glass so that the string is pulled tight. Carefully begin to pour water into the glass. The water will cling to the string and flow along it into the glass.

How to Defy Gravity

Continue to pour water along the string while you slowly move the cup away from the pitcher. Keep the string tight, don't pour too quickly and the water will follow the string.

How to Make the Puffa-chute Cone

1. Fold the paper in half. Holding the paper steady at the centre of the fold, grasp the bottom left corner of the paper and twist it into a cone as shown.

2. Adjust the diameter of the open end of the cone so that it is slightly bigger than the diameter of the cardboard tube. Tape the cone so it doesn't unwind.

3. Slide the cone, nose first, into the tube until it will slide no farther. Cut off any of the cone that's sticking out of the tube. Remove the cone from the tube.

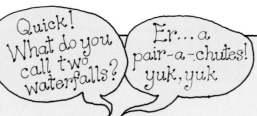

Things you'll need:
piece of notebook-size paper; scissors; sticky tape; plastic bag; cotton thread; 30 cm (12 inches) length of cardboard wrapping paper tube

Quick! What do you call two waterfalls?

Er...a pair-a-chutes! yuk, yuk

About this experiment:
Dr. Zed looks at air pressure as well as the effects of air resistance on a large surface.

I love Puffa-chuting, especially the floating down part.

When the chute opens up it has to move so much air out of the way that the air piles up underneath it and acts as a brake.

How to Launch Your Puffa-chute

1. Slide the cone, open end first, into the cardboard tube until none of it is sticking out.

2. Place the loaded end of the tube in the centre of the chute and gather the ends of the chute around the tube.

3. As you blow hard into the open end of the tube, let go of the plastic chute.

How to Make the Plastic Chute

1. Cut a 24 cm x 24 cm (9-1/2 inches x 9-1/2 inches) square out of the plastic bag.

2. Cut four threads 24 cm (9-1/2 inches) long and tie one to each corner of the plastic square.

3. Knot the four loose ends of thread together and tape to the nose of the paper cone.

Did you know that 16 million million million atoms rush to join a sugar crystal every hour?

That's what I call a rush-hour!

About this experiment:

Dr. Zed examines crystal formation in a supersaturated sugar solution.

How to Make Your Crystal Pops

1. Mix the sugar and water in the pot and heat it on the stove, stirring until the sugar dissolves. Boil the mixture for one minute.

2. Take the pot off the stove. When the mixture is cool, pour it into the glass or jar.

3. Put a popsicle stick in the jar and leave it uncovered in a warm room until large crystals start to form. This will take about a week.

If a crust forms, break it and gather the floating crystals on to your popsicle stick.

I'm impressed. when can I eat it?

Go back to sleep. We'll wake you when it's ready. Tee hee.

Tina Holdcroft

35

DR. ZED'S SEE-ALL CAT'S EYES

Tab A

Eye strip

SLIT A

Cut out dotted circle

Cut out dotted circle

How to Make Your See-All Cat's Eyes:

1. Trace and colour the cat's face and the eye strip next to it. Cut along slits A and B.

2. Working from the back of the cat's face, push tab A through slit A, and tab B through slit B.

3. When you turn the face over you should see eyes in the circles and there should be a space between the eye strip and the back of the face.

4. Hang the cat's face at eye level, then move at least 3 m (10 feet) away. As you walk about, watch what the cat's eyes do.

Run! It's a cat!

Tab B

About this experiment:
Dr. Zed investigates optical
illusions created by objects on
different planes and seen from
different angles.

Why do witches fly on brooms?

Because vacuum cleaners are too heavy!

It can't be watching all of us! What's happening, Dr. Zed?

When you move to one side of the cat, the eyeholes frame a different section of the continuous eyestrip, making the pupils appear to turn towards you.

But you were the only one that moved.

No! No! It's watching me!

It's watching me!

..Tina Holdcroft...

DR. ZED ASKS "DO YOU HAVE ESP?"

I know what it is! I know!

Hmph! If you've got ESP, I'm a UFO.

I'm getting a strong image... it's a, it's a duck!

How to Make Your ESP Cards

1. Divide the cardboard into 25 rectangles, all the same size.

2. Mark five of the cards with a square, five with a cross, five with a circle, five with a star and five with wavy lines. *(See examples in photo.)*

3. Draw all five symbols on a large sheet of paper.

How to Test a Friend for ESP

1. Shuffle the cards and place face down on the table. Look at the top card, making sure that no one else can see it.

2. Try to send a mental image of the symbol to your friend and ask her to name the symbol.

3. Place the card face down on the sheet of paper, next to the symbol your friend named.

4. Go through all 25 cards in this way.

How to Collect Data

1. At the end of the test see how many cards match the symbols.

2. Most people make five correct guesses. If your friend got more than five correct, repeat the experiment many times, recording the score each time. At the end, add up the number of correct guesses, divide by the number of times you repeated the experiment and if the result is more than five, ESP might be at work.

Things you'll need:

two egg whites; 2 mL (1/2 tsp) vanilla; 2 mL (1/2 tsp) vinegar; 50 mL (1/4 cup) sugar; 125 mL (1/2 cup) chocolate chips; cookie sheets; aluminum foil; glass bowl; measuring cups and spoons; mixer or wire whisk; spoon

What kind of tests do chickens write?

Eggs-ams! How's that for a good yolk?

About this experiment:

Dr. Zed examines how proteins react to the stress of being mixed and heated.

Egg whites are mostly protein. Beating changes the shape of the protein molecules so they can trap air and expand to three times their original size. The more air you beat in, the foamier the whites get.

How to Make Your Meringues

1. Take the eggs out of the refrigerator so that they'll warm up to room temperature. Preheat the oven to 120°C (250°F). Cover the cookie sheets with foil, dull side up.

2. Place the egg whites, vanilla and vinegar in the bowl. Using the mixer or wire whisk, whip the mixture until it is white and frothy.

3. Beat in the sugar a little at a time until you've added it all. Keep whipping the mixture until it's stiff and glossy.

4. Lightly stir in the chocolate chips.

5. Drop the batter by spoonfuls onto the cookie sheets and bake for about one hour, until the cookies are light brown. Let them cool before removing from the sheets.

Makes two dozen.

Why do the egg whites change from liquid to foam, Dr. Zed?

41

How to Make Your Moving Mouse Machine

1. Mark cardboard like this:

10 cm (4 inches)

3.5 cm (1-3/8 inch)

Each slot is 5 cm (2 inches) long, 6 cm (1/4 inch) wide and 6 cm (1/4 inch) from the top. Cut 10.

.6 cm (1/4 inch) tab for gluing

35.5 cm (14 inches)

2. Ask an adult to help you cut out the 10 slots.

Tab

Things you'll need:

35.5 cm x 10 cm (14 inches x 4 inches) rectangle thin cardboard; scissors; **sharp knife** *(ask permission to use this)*; **pencil; ruler; tracing paper; paper; glue; turntable**

Did you know that Dr. Zed's 'moving mouse machine' was invented more than 150 years ago?

Really? He doesn't look that old!

About this experiment:

Dr. Zed explores persistence of vision.

Not moving? What does he mean, Dr. Zed?

He's right! Your brain continues to see each picture one-tenth of a second after it's disappeared. Since the cylinder is turning quickly, your brain overlaps the images so it looks as if the mouse is somersaulting.

3. Trace the two strips of mouse drawings below. Join the strips together to form a continuous loop with the mouse drawings inside.

4. Assemble the moving mouse machine so that it looks like this:

Lights, Camera, Action...

Stand your moving mouse machine on the turntable, making sure that it's centred. Switch on the turntable to 33 rpm and look through the slots so you can see the revolving pictures.

Can you see the mouse flip?

Tab

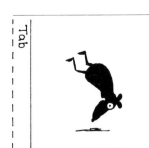 

43

DR. ZED'S SATELLITE BALLOON

How to Make Your Satellite Balloon

1. Blow up the balloon and knot it.

2. Fill a large basin with cold water and ice.

3. Fill several plastic cups with the hottest water you can get out of the tap. Watch your fingers!

4. Empty out one cup into the sink. Quickly press the open end of the cup against the balloon.

5. Holding the cup firmly against the balloon, immediately dip the cup into the basin of ice water. Hold it there 20 seconds.

6. Let go of the cup and it will stay in place.

7. Stick on as many cups as you can in this way.

N.B. If you can't get your cup to stick to the balloon, either the water isn't hot or cold enough or you're not working fast enough.

DATE:	EXPERIMENT:

NOTES:

Index

ABOUT THE AUTHOR

Gordon Penrose, the zany Dr. Zed, is regularly featured in OWL, the international magazine for children, and on OWL/TV, the childrens' discovery program broadcast throughout North America. A retired Master Teacher of Science, Gordon now travels extensively, giving science workshops for children and educators. This is his third science activity book.

Dr. Zed's philosophy, like that of OWL Magazine, is that learning can be fun. Because it is important for children to discover for themselves, all the activities in this book encourage creative experimentation, and while each one focuses on one major science understanding, it touches on others as well. All the activities have been tested with children, can be carried out with a minimum of adult supervision, and are designed to be suitable for both home and classroom.